Learn this rhyme

Good Morning!
Good morning! Good morning!
   Good morning! How are you?
Good morning! Good morning!
   Good morning! How are you?
The sun is shining, birds are singing,
   And the sky is blue.
Good morning! Good morning!
   Good morning! How are you?

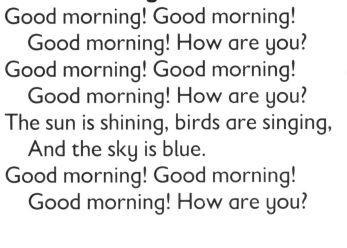

Revision

2 Look and act

Learn these rhymes

Good Afternoon!
Good afternoon! Good afternoon!
　　How are you today?
It's twelve o'clock. We're eating lunch.
　　Please sit down and stay.
Look at the sky. The sun is high.
　　Now it's time to play!
Good afternoon! Good afternoon!
　　How are you today?

Goodbye!
I'm fine, thanks. I'm fine, thanks.
　　I'm very well today.
I'm fine, thanks. I'm fine, thanks.
　　I'm sorry I can't stay.
I'm going to school. Look at the clock!
　　I haven't time to play.
Goodbye! Goodbye!
　　Sorry I can't stay.

Revision

4 **A puzzle**

Can you see these?   Point and say.
a leaf, a star, a snake, a fly, a ball, a cap, a knife,
a plate, a spoon, a doll, a glass, an ice-cream, a button,
a gate

What can you see?

Sam: Look at this.
Susan: What is it?
Sam: It's a _____.
Susan: Yes, and this is a _____.

Can you see these?
a bird, a ladder, a hen, an elephant, a bus, a horse,
a fish, a goat, a flower, a boat, a cat a car, a bell,
a dog, a train

Revision

6 What are they saying?

fat   thin   short   tall

1a. Look at me! I'm _____!

Look at me! I'm _____!

1b.

1c. Look at me! I'm _____!

Look at me! I'm _____!

1d.

2   h. I'm _____!   g. I'm _____!   f. I'm _____!   e. I'm _____!

a. I'm happy.   b. I'm sad.   c. I'm _____!   d. I'm _____!

Revision

What are they saying?

1

2a.

2b.

2c.

2d.

Revision

8 One word is different. Say it.

1

a cinema   a post office   <u>a table</u>   a school

2

father   mother   sailor   brother   daughter

3

a nose   an ear   a mouth   a shirt

4

a doctor   a tree   a farmer   a nurse

5

a pen   a chair   a pencil   a rubber

6

a hen   a box   a cat   a dog

Revision

There's a mouse in the flat!   Where is it?

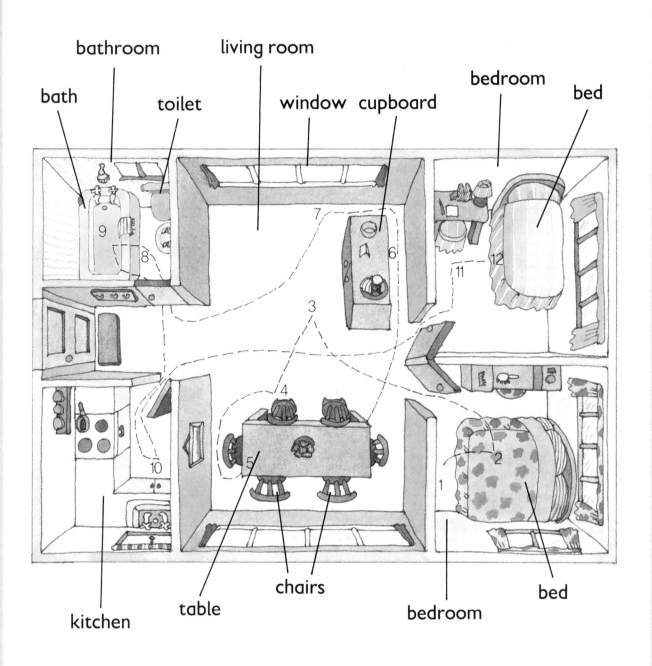

bathroom

living room

bedroom

bed

bath

toilet

window   cupboard

kitchen

table

chairs

bedroom

bed

1   It's in a bedroom.
2   Now it's on the bed.
3   Now it's in the . . .

A puzzle

Ask or answer the questions:

1 Who's cooking? __ cocinando
2 Who's drinking? -- bebiendo
3 Who's swimming?
4 Who's running?
5 Who's sleeping?
6 Who's eating?
7 Who's crying?
8 Who's riding a bicycle?

9 Who's flying an aeroplane?
10 Who's hopping?
11 Who's painting?
12 Who's jumping?
13 Who's singing?
14 Who's cutting?
15 Who's walking?
16 Who's driving a car?

Mary   Mike   Ann   Teresa   Sarah   Susan

Helen   Peter   John   Mabel   David   Mark

Tom   Sam   Tim   Linda

Revision

What are they saying?

aeroplane
300

bag
5

doll
10

boat
5

kite
4

football
50

bicycle
500

radio
200

book
10

car
4

John: There's a _____ in the window.

Mary: Where?

John: In
On
Behind the _____.
Near
Under

Mary: Can we buy it?

John: No, it's expensive.
Yes, it's cheap.

Mary: How much is it?

John: It's _____.

Revision

12 A puzzle

Where are these?

The bus-driver's head.
The policeman's arm.
The old man's hand.

The woman's foot.
The baby's face.
The girl's leg.

A number puzzle

How many triangles?
Count in English.

There are eighty-five triangles.
Can you find them?

Revision

14

What is wrong in the picture?

There is a hen on the door.
The teacher is holding an umbrella.
A girl has a telephone.

Revision

Read and act

Revision

coffee

tea

bread

butter

sugar

ice-cream

milk

salt

jam

soup

rice

water

1

2

3

	Mary	Mike	Susan	Sarah	Sam	John	
coffee		✓				✓	
tea	✓			✓	✓		
bread							
butter			✓				
sugar			✓				
ice-cream	✓	✓		✓			
milk			✓				
salt							
jam	✓			✓	✓		
soup		✓				✓	
rice							
water							

Read:

coffee:	Mike and John like coffee.
tea:	Mary, Sarah and Sam like tea.
bread:	No one likes bread.
sugar:	Susan likes sugar.
ice-cream:	Mary, Mike, and Sarah like ice-cream.
milk:	Susan likes milk.
salt:	No one likes salt.
jam:	Mary, Sarah and Sam like jam.
soup:	Mike and John like soup.

A *Make five true sentences beginning:*

I like . . .

B *Make five true sentences beginning:*

I don't like . . .

C *Make five true sentences beginning with the names of your friends:*

Sam likes . . .

Mary likes . . .

Sarah likes . . .

Read aloud:

a

an apple   a bag   a cat

e

a bed   a desk   an egg

i

a finger   milk   a pin

o

a bottle   a clock   a dog

u

a bus   a cup   a duck

Revision

4

Can I have a packet of tea, please?

I'm sorry, sir. I don't sell tea.

5

You don't sell bread.
You don't sell coffee.
You don't sell tea.
You don't sell butter.
What do you sell?

I sell fish, sir.
This is a fish shop.
You are in the wrong shop!

Read:

You can buy fish in a fish shop.
You cannot buy bread.
You cannot buy coffee.
You cannot buy tea.
You cannot buy butter.

1

This is the way I
   wash my hands,
   wash my hands,
   wash my hands.
This is the way I
   wash my hands,
Early in the morning.

That is the way he
   washes his hands,
   washes his hands,
   washes his hands.
That is the way he
   washes his hands,
Early in the morning.

2

28

A *Finish these sentences:*

1 A book shop sells . . .

2 A shoe shop sells . . .

3 A hat shop . . .

4 A dress shop . . .

5 A radio shop . . .

6 A camera shop . . .

B *How many sentences can you make?*

1 You cannot buy a book in a shoe shop.

2 You cannot buy a shoe in a hat shop.

3 You cannot buy a hat in . . . .

Read aloud:

a

a hand   a man   jam

e

a leg   a pen   red

i

a pin   a ship   a window

o

a doll   an orange   a doctor

u

a rubber   the sun   an umbrella

Revision

1 Can you swim, Sam?

Can you cook, Sam?

2 Can you sing, Susan?

Can you ride a bicycle, Susan?

3 Can you play football, Mike?

Can you play the piano, Mike?

4 Can you ride a bicycle, Mary?   Can you ride a horse, Mary?

5 Can you drive a car, Mr. Lake?   Can you fly an aeroplane, Mr. Lake?

6 Can you stand on one leg, John?   Can you stand on your head, John?

Read:

1 Sam can swim
but he cannot cook.

2 Susan can sing
but she cannot ride
a bicycle.

3 Mike can play football
but he cannot play
the piano.

4 Mary can ride a bicycle
but she cannot ride
a horse.

5 Mr. Lake can drive a car
but he cannot fly
an aeroplane.

6 John can stand on one leg
but he cannot stand
on his head.

Read aloud:
(Make the sounds long.)

a

a page   a face   a plate

e

he   me   we

i

a line   a knife   nine

o

a stove   a nose   a home

u

a ruler   blue   Susan

34

A rhyme to learn:

Don't run across the road.
Stop and look.

Don't write on the wall.
Write in your book.

Don't run in school.
Always walk.

Listen to the teacher.
Please don't talk.

A *Finish the sentences with* **can** *or* **cannot**.

1 A fish _____ swim.

2 A dog _____ swim.

3 A cat _____ swim.

4 A bird _____ fly.

5 A mouse _____ fly.

6 A bird _____ sing.

7 A dog _____ stand on one leg.

8 A hen _____ stand on one leg.

B *Finish the sentences with* **is** *or* **are**.

1 Ice-cream _____ cold but fire _____ hot.

2 Grass _____ green but the sky _____ blue.

3 Trees _____ big but matches _____ small.

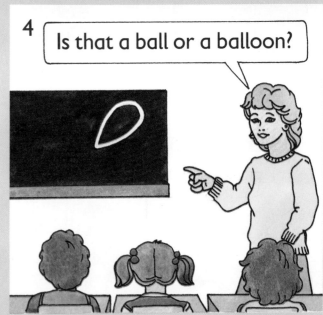

38 What is this?

1

Is this a shoe
or a boot?

2

Is this a box
or a basket?

3

Is this an apple
or an orange?

4

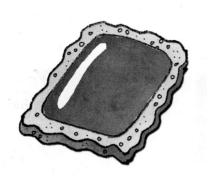

Is this a biscuit
or a cake?

5

Is this a bus
or a lorry?

6

Is this a river
or a road?

7

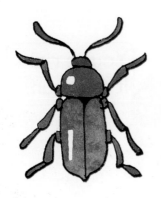

Is this a fly
or a cockroach?

8

Is this a fork
or a knife?

9

Is this a shirt
or a tie?

Answer these questions:

1 Are you a boy or a girl?

2 Is your teacher a man or a woman?

3 Is the Head of your school a man or a woman?

4 Is your school big or small?

5 Is your home in a town or a village?

6 Is your school quiet or noisy?

Read aloud:

ea = ee

the sea · a seat

tea

read

eat

clean

But:

a head · bread

Read aloud:

oo (long)

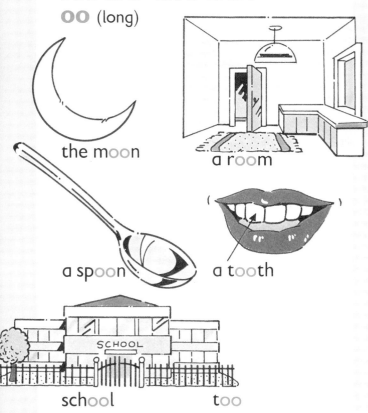

the moon

a room

a spoon

a tooth

school

too

Read aloud:

oo (short)

the book

a cook

a foot

good

look

A *Answer the questions.*

1 Is ice cold or hot?

2 Is a mouse big or small?

3 Is a page of a book thin or thick?

4 Is the sun hot or cold?

5 Is the moon hot or cold?

6 Is milk black or white?

B *Answer the questions.*

1 Are you writing with a pen or pencil?

2 Is this the top of the page or the bottom?

Revision

7

8

9

10

Do you know these?

rabbits

cows

monkeys

bees

Read aloud:

c = s

a face

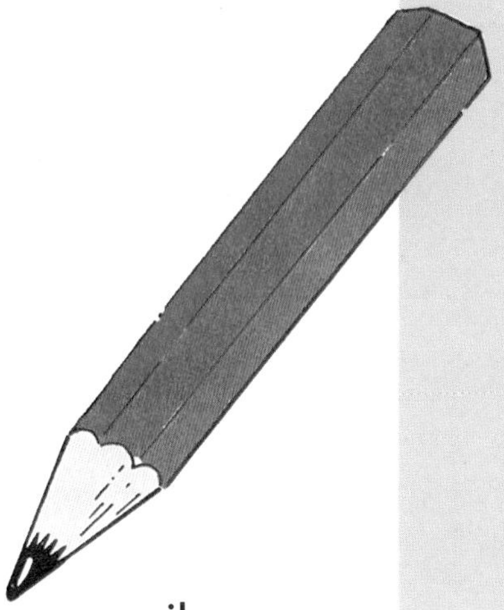

a pencil

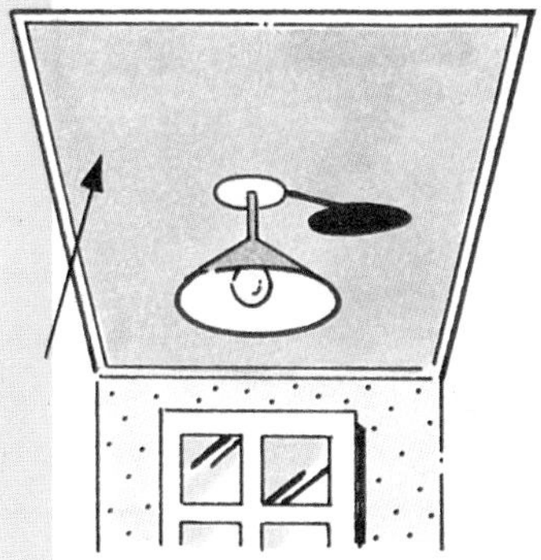

a ceiling

a circle

a bicycle

a cinema

an ice-cream

rice

Look at the postman in the street.
  Can you see him?
  I can see him.
Look at the woman on the seat.
  Can you see her?
  I can see her.

Look at the aeroplane in the sky.
  Can you see it?
  I can see it.
Look at the clouds. They're very high.
  Can you see them?
  I can see them.

Look at the bird in the tree.
  Can you see it?
  I can see it.
Look at the children in the sea.
  Can you see them?
  I can see them.

Look at the driver of the bus.
  Can you see him?
  I can see him.
We can see him but he can't see us!
  Can you see him?
  I can see him.

Read the question. Then point at the right sign or signal and say 'This one' or 'That one'.

Questions:

1 Which one means 'Do not turn right'?

2 Which one means 'Do not turn left'?

3 Which one means 'Do not walk across the road now'?

4 Which one means 'Do not ride a bicycle'?

5 Which one means 'Men's toilet'?

6 Which one means 'Ladies' toilet'?

7 Which one means 'I am turning right'?

8 Which one means 'Walk across the road now'?

9 Which one means 'Do not walk here'?

10 Which one means 'Turn right'?

11 Which one means 'I am turning left'?

12 Which one means 'Do not touch'?

13 Which one means 'Do not go in here'?

14 Which one means 'No buses'?

15 Which one means 'There is a telephone here'?

Read the question. Then point at the right sign and say 'This one' or 'That one'.

1. Which one means 'Do not smoke'?
2. Which one means 'This is the way out'?
3. Which one means 'Do not make a noise'?
4. Which one means 'You can catch a bus here'?
5. Which one means 'School children cross the road here'?
6. Which one means 'You can leave your car here'?
7. Which one means 'This is the way in'?
8. Which one means 'Do not drink this'?
9. Which one means 'Be careful'?

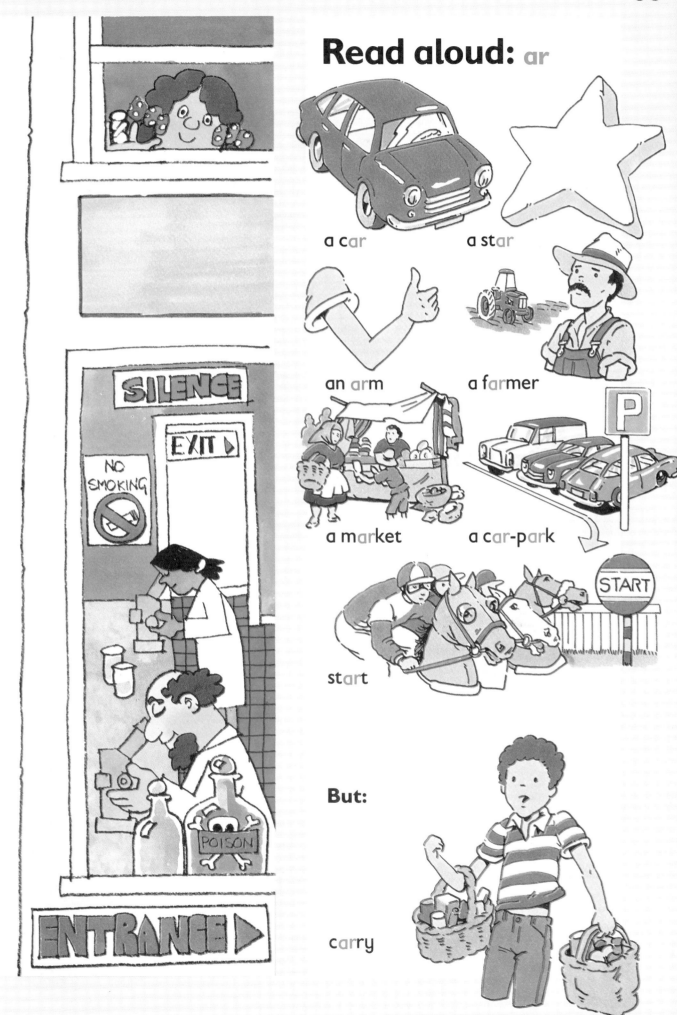

Read aloud: ar

a car

a star

an arm

a farmer

a market

a car-park

start

But:

carry

A *Ask your teacher for three things. Begin: May I . . . ?*

B *Choose the right word:*

1 Sam is working and I am helping _____.
(him/her/it)

2 Miss Lake is talking and we are listening to _____.
(him/her/it)

3 Where is my pencil? Can you see _____?
(them/him/it)

4 The boys are in the room. I can see _____.
(him/it/them)

5 We are sitting in the classroom. The teacher is talking to_____.
(we/us/them)

6 I am talking to the dog but it is not listening to _____.
(me/it/him)

Read aloud: ai

a train   rain

paint   a tail

wait   again

But:

a chair   hair

A poem to learn

Say it quietly to a friend but shout the last word!

In a dark wood

There's a dark house.

In the dark house

There's a dark room.

In the dark room

There's a dark cupboard.

In the dark cupboard

There's a dark shelf.

On the dark shelf

There's a dark box.

In the dark box

There's a GHOST!

58

Choose a name for each picture:

a. An angry bus-driver.
b. A beautiful flower.
c. A bad drawing.
d. An ugly face.
e. A heavy box.
f. A rich woman.
g. A tall soldier.
h. An old man.
i. A happy child.
j. A lazy boy.
k. A lovely girl.
l. A dirty cat.
m. A clean plate.
n. A big elephant.
o. A thin horse.
p. A pretty dress.
q. A short sailor.
r. A young boy.

Choose a name for each picture. Be careful.

a. A hot day.
b. A cold day.
c. A sunny day.
d. A rainy day.
e. A thirsty dog.
f. A hungry dog.
g. A short dress.
h. A long dress.
i. A new car.
j. An old car.
k. A cheap camera.
l. An expensive camera.
m. A strong man.
n. A weak man.
o. A thick book.
p. A thin book.

1

2

5

6

8

9

10

13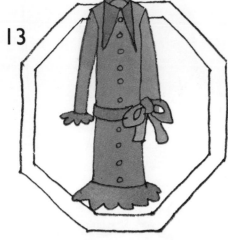

14

15

Read aloud: ow

down	town
brown	cow
how	now

Read aloud: ow

yellow	window
know	

Read aloud: ow

flower

1

2

That's not our ball.
This is our ball.

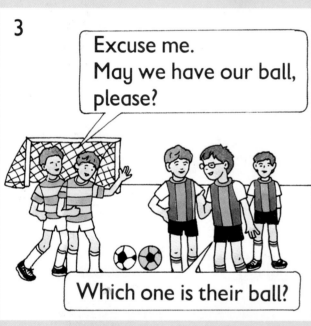

3

Excuse me.
May we have our ball, please?

Which one is their ball?

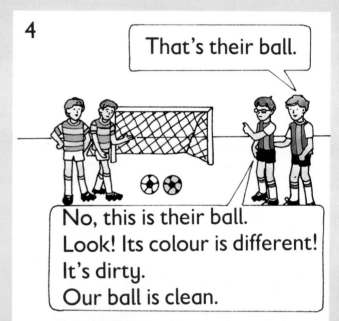

4

That's their ball.

No, this is their ball.
Look! Its colour is different!
It's dirty.
Our ball is clean.

5

Thank you.
I'm sorry we stopped your game.

That's all right.
Come on, John!

6

Wait, Sam!
What are you doing?

I'm scoring a goal!

> That's the wrong goal, Sam!
> That's our goal!
> This is their goal!

7

63

A *Look at these signs.*

1 Which one means 'Do not smoke'?
2 Which one means 'Do not touch'?
3 Which one means 'Do not walk here'?
4 Which one means 'Danger'?

1    2

3    4

B *What are these?*

1    2

3    4

1 A _____ car.

Revision

We are David and Jane.
Our family name is Taylor.
Our father is Mr. Donald Taylor.
Our mother is Mrs. Rita Taylor
We have three young brothers.
Their names are Alan, Bernard and Colin.
Their ages are three, five and seven.
We have a dog, too.
Its name is Wolf.

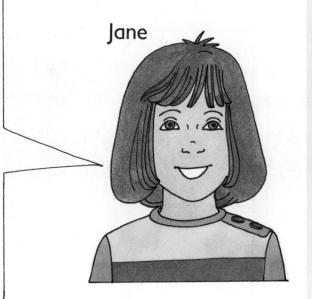

Jane

David

This is our home.   These are our flats.

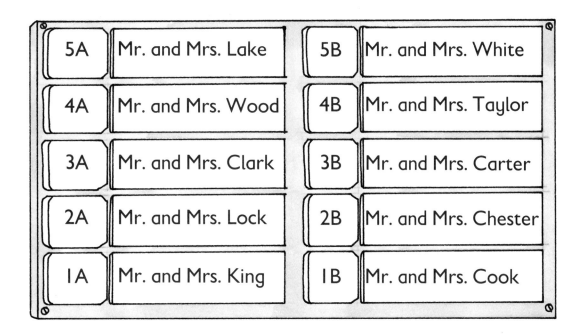

5A	Mr. and Mrs. Lake	5B	Mr. and Mrs. White
4A	Mr. and Mrs. Wood	4B	Mr. and Mrs. Taylor
3A	Mr. and Mrs. Clark	3B	Mr. and Mrs. Carter
2A	Mr. and Mrs. Lock	2B	Mr. and Mrs. Chester
1A	Mr. and Mrs. King	1B	Mr. and Mrs. Cook

Our flat is between Mr. and Mrs. White's flat and
   Mr. and Mrs. Carter's flat.
The Whites are our friends.
Their flat is above us.
The Carters are our friends, too.
Their flat is under us.
The Cooks are our friends, too.
Their flat is under Mr. and Mrs. Chester's flat.

A   *Answer these questions:*
1 Where is Mr. and Mrs. Lake's flat?   Their flat is . . .
2 Where is Mr. and Mrs. Wood's flat?
3 Where is Mr. and Mrs. Clark's flat?
4 Where is Mr. and Mrs. King's flat?
5 Where is Mr. and Mrs. Cook's flat?
6 Where is Mr. and Mrs. Lock's flat?

B *Can you draw your flats?*

C *Can you write the names of some of the people?*

Answer the questions:

A *Where can I buy it?*

1 Where can I buy some biscuits?
   There are some biscuits in Lake's store but
   there aren't any in Carter's shop.

2 Where can I buy some jam?
   There is some jam in Carter's shop but
   there isn't any in Lake's store.

3 Where can I buy some sweets?
   There are . . . .

4 Where can I buy some milk?
   There is . . . .

5 Where can I buy some eggs?
   There are . . . .

6 Where can I buy some soup?
   There is . . . .

B *Can you add things to these lists?*

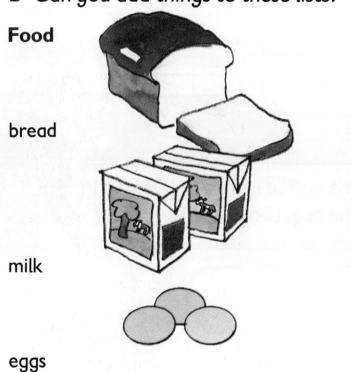

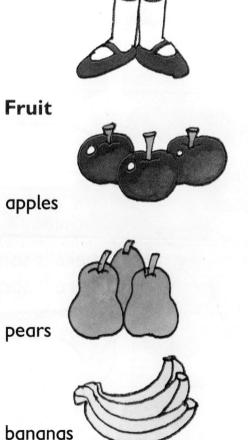

Food

bread

milk

eggs

Fruit

apples

pears

bananas

Clothes

shoes

a shirt

socks

trousers

Furniture

a table

a chair

Read aloud: ou

a house

a cloud

a mouth

round

trousers

loud

shout

about

But:

touch

colour

young

Marco goes to school by train.

Chieko goes to school by car.

Mike goes to school by bus.

Maria goes to school on foot.

Ada goes to school by bicycle.

A *Read:*

Marco lives in Europe.
He gets up at ten to seven.
He goes to school by train.

Mike lives in North America.
He gets up at five to seven.
He goes to school by bus.

B *Now make three sentences for Chieko, Maria, and Ada.*

C *Finish these sentences:*

1 My home is . . . .

2 I live . . . .

3 I get up . . . .

4 I go to school . . . .

D *A rhyme to learn:*

Some people go to school by bus.

Some people go by train.

Some go by car,　　some go on foot,

But no one goes by plane.

1

2

3

4

5

a dentist

a fisherman

a postman

a farmer

a workman

a doctor

a sailor

a fireman

a policeman

a soldier

a driver

a teacher

a shopkeeper

an office-worker

a factory-worker

76

Read aloud: er

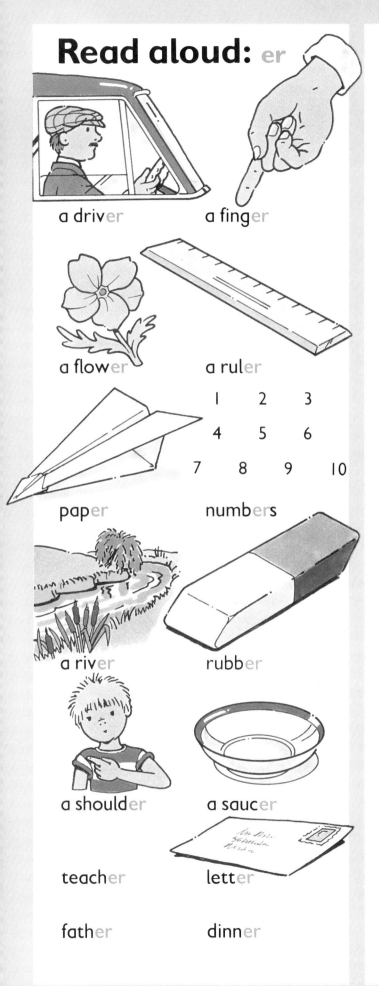

a driv**er**   a fing**er**

a flow**er**   a rul**er**

1	2	3
4	5	6
7	8	9	10

pap**er**   numb**er**s

a riv**er**   rubb**er**

a should**er**   a sauc**er**

teach**er**   lett**er**

fath**er**   dinn**er**

A *Choose the true answer:*

1 Have you any brothers?
  a. No, I haven't any brothers.
  b. Yes, I have a brother.
  c. Yes, I have some brothers.

2 Have you any sisters?
  a. No, I haven't any sisters.
  b. Yes, I have a sister.
  c. Yes, I have some sisters.

B *Choose a friend and finish these sentences:*

1 My friend's name is . . .
2 He/She lives . . .
3 He/She gets up . . .
4 He/She goes to school . . .

C *Finish these sentences ;*

1 He works on a farm. He is a _____ .
2 He drives a bus. He is a _____ .
3 She works in an office. She is an _____ .

Revision

A week

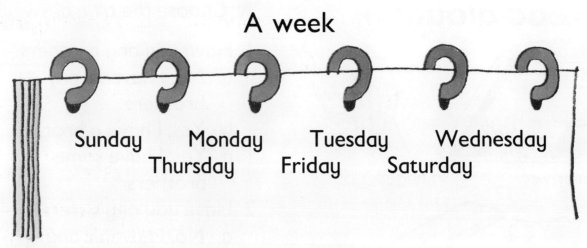

Sunday   Monday   Tuesday   Wednesday
Thursday   Friday   Saturday

1 How many days are there in a week?
2 Which day comes before Wednesday?
3 Which day comes after Friday?
4 Which days are school days?
5 What is today?
6 What is tomorrow?
7 How many letters are there in Wednesday?
8 Can you close the book and spell Thursday, Wednesday and Saturday?

The months

January   February   March   April

May   June   July   August

September   October   November   December

Can you spell them?

How many days are there in a month? Learn this rhyme.

There are thirty days in September,
  April, June and November.
All the others have thirty-one
  Except February.

When is your birthday? It is on one of these days:

The	first, second, third, fourth, fifth, sixth, seventh, eighth, ninth, tenth, eleventh, twelfth, thirteenth, fourteenth, fifteenth, sixteenth, seventeenth, eighteenth, nineteenth, twentieth, twenty-first, twenty-second, twenty-third, twenty-fourth, twenty-fifth, twenty-sixth, twenty-seventh, twenty-eighth, twenty-ninth, thirtieth, thirty-first	of	January. February. March. April. May. June. July. August. September. October. November. December.

My birthday is on . . . .

My friend's birthday is on . . . .

My mother's birthday is on . . . .

Answer these questions:

1 Which day of the week is it today?

2 What is the date today?

3 Which day of the week is it tomorrow?

4 What is the date tomorrow?

5 Which day was it yesterday?

6 Which month is it now?

7 Which year is it now?

8 How many days are there in January?

9 How many days are there in June?

10 How many days are there in the second month?

11 How many days are there in the ninth month?

12 How many weeks are there in one month?

13 Whose birthday is today?

14 Whose birthday is tomorrow?

Read aloud: o = u

January
February
March

months	colours
Monday	others
mother	brother
above	some

Read aloud: au

August	saucer
daughter	naughty

But:

laugh

wet   cloudy   dry   sunny

hot   warm   cool   cold

1 What is the weather in our town today?

Today it is
- wet
- cloudy
- dry
- sunny

and
- hot.
- warm.
- cool.
- cold.

2 What was the weather yesterday?

Yesterday it was
- wet
- cloudy
- dry
- sunny

and
- hot.
- warm.
- cool.
- cold.

3 What was the weather last January?   Last January it was . .

4 What was the weather last April?

5 What was the weather last August?

6 What was the weather last November?

I

84

2

3

What is different?

The ruler was on the chair. Now
   it's on the table.
The rubber was on the chair. Now
   it's on the table.
The bottle was on the floor. Now
   it's on the table.
The book was on the table. Now
   it's on the chair.
The pencil was on the table. Now
   it's on the chair.
The knife was on the table. Now
   it's on the floor.
The clock was on the table. Now
   it's on the chair.

4

No, the clock wasn't on the table.
It was on the floor.

Yes, that's right.
Now, I remember.

5

Where were the shoe, the box, and the hat?

They were . . . They were . . .
I can't remember.
Wait!
The shoe and the box were on the chair.

6

No, they weren't.
They were on the floor.
Where was the hat?

It was . . . It was . . .
I can't remember.
Wait!
It was on the floor, too!

7

That's right.
Good!
Seven of your answers were right.
That's very good!

Thank you.

1 Which day is it today?

2 What is today's date?

3 What was yesterday's date?

4 How many days are there in a week?

5 How many months are there in a year?

6 Spell the fourth day of the week.

7 Spell the second month.

8 Spell the eighth month.

9 How many days are there in April?

10 How many days are there in March?

11 What was the date last Saturday?

12 What was the weather last Saturday?

13 How many children are there in your class today?

14 How many children were there in your class yesterday?

Read aloud: ir

a girl a bird

a shirt a skirt

a dirty shirt

Read aloud: ur

a nurse

Thursday Saturday

turn

Revision

Sing or say this English children's song:

Old Macdonald's Farm

1

Old Macdonald had a farm,
E — I — E — I — O,
And on his farm he had some ducks,
E — I — E — I — O,
With a quack-quack here
And a quack-quack there,
Here a quack, there a quack,
Everywhere a quack-quack.
Old Macdonald had a farm,
E — I — E — I — O.

2

Old Macdonald had a farm,
E — I — E — I — O.
And on his farm he had some cows,
E — I — E — I — O,
With a moo-moo here
And a moo-moo there,
Here a moo, there a moo,
Everywhere a moo-moo.
With a quack-quack here
And a quack-quack there,
Here a quack, there a quack,
Everywhere a quack-quack.
Old Macdonald had a farm,
E — I — E — I — O.

3

Old Macdonald had a farm,
E — I — E — I — O,
And on his farm he had some sheep,
E — I — E — I — O,
With a baa-baa here
And a baa-baa there,
Here a baa, there a baa,
Everywhere a baa-baa.
With a moo-moo here
And a moo-moo there,
Here a moo, there a moo,
Everywhere a moo-moo.
With a quack-quack here
And a quack-quack there,
Here a quack, there a quack,
Everywhere a quack-quack.
Old Macdonald had a farm,
E — I — E — I — O.

4

Old Macdonald had a farm,
E — I — E — I — O,
And on his farm he had some hens,
E — I — E — I — O,
With a cluck-cluck here
And a cluck-cluck there,
Here a cluck, there a cluck . . .

Some problems

1

I had five apples
but I was hungry.
I ate two.
How many have I got now?

2

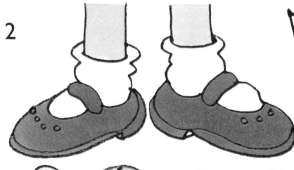

I had twelve eggs
but I was careless.
I dropped four.
How many have I got now?

3

I had eight cakes
but I was greedy.
I ate six.
How many have I got now?

4

I had nine coins
but I was careless.
I lost four.
How many have I got now?

5

I had ten oranges.

I ate four.

I lost two.

My mother gave me
two coins.

I bought five oranges.

I ate one.

How many have I got?

Read aloud: or

40

forty   morning

a horse   a fork

or   for

short   story

Read aloud: or = er

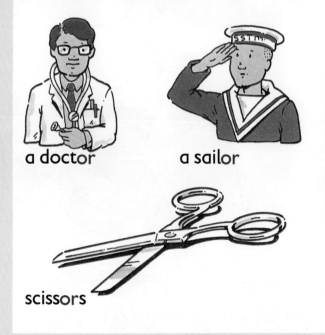

a doctor   a sailor

scissors

Sam played football.

Mary cleaned the flat.

Mike watched television.

John made a kite.

Sarah washed her hair.

Susan wrote a letter.

Ann went to the market.

Patrick helped his father.

David had a swim.

Jane walked in the country.

Tom bought a radio.

Last Saturday I . . .

Read aloud:

tr

a train

a tractor

a tree

trousers

dr

a dress

a drum

a drawer

drinking

gr

grass

green

grey

grandfather
grandson

br

bread

brown

a brush

brother
bring
breakfast

fl

a fly

a flower

flour

the floor

cl

a clock

a cloud

clothes

clean
class
close

Roll over!

There were five in the bed
And the little one said,
'Roll over, roll over.'
So they all rolled over,
And one fell out.

There were four in the bed
And the little one said,
'Roll over, roll over.'
So they all rolled over,
And one fell out.

There were three in the bed
And the little one said,
'Roll over, roll over.'
So they all rolled over,
And one fell out.

There were two in the bed
And the little one said,
'Roll over, roll over.'
So they all rolled over,
And one fell out.

There was one in the bed
And the little one said,
'Good night!'

The items in the two lists below are included in this book. The numbers refer to the pages on which the items occur. The word 'throughout' means that the item occurs too often to be listed.

Communicative functions

Greetings, response to greetings, farewell: 1–3, 19, 34, 94
The time: 3, 71, 73; the day and the date: 78–81
Counting: 13
Saying the letters of the alphabet and spelling: throughout
The weather: 82–84, 86
Identifying and describing simple objects: throughout
Simple descriptions of themselves and others: 6–8, 29–31, 63, 67, 73–77, 79, 80
What people are doing: 3, 10, 14, 34, 43, 62
Asking and answering questions about location: 9, 11, 14, 70–33

Asking and answering questions about personal possessions: 15, 39, 62, 63
Asking what things are in English: 37–39, 74, 75
Making simple enquiries about a person: 1–3, 15, 74–77
Asking permission to do simple things: 34, 56
Requesting things needed: 23, 24, 44, 56, 62
Making and responding to an apology or excuse: 3, 21, 23, 62
Thanks: 2, 62
Likes, dislikes, needs and wants: 19–21, 40, 42, 66, 67

Responding to instructions: throughout; giving instructions: 3, 5, 6, 32, 33, 35
Inability to respond: 45
Oral and written prohibitions and injunctions: 32–33, 35, 52–55, 65
Comprehending simple narratives: 19–21, 23–24, 32–34, 40–42, 62–63, 89, 91–92
Recognizing common signs: 52–55
English names of important places: 70, 73

Language items

Formula expressions
Common greetings, farewells, etc: 1–3, 19, 34
please: 15, 19, 23, 35, 36, 37, 40–42, 44; *thanks/thank you*: 2, 3, 40, 41, 44; *yes, please*: 41; *no, thank you*: 42; *I'm sorry*: 3, 21, 23, 45; *certainly*: 19, 40; *that's all right*: 62; *excuse me*: 62

Adjectives
Possessive : 15, 25–27, 30, 31, 39, 48, 49, 62–66
Predicative: 1–3, 6, 11, 14, 21, 43, 62, 65, 82, 83, 86, 89
Attributive: 19–21, 24, 57, 58–61, 63, 94
Demonstrative: *that*: 34; *those*; 34, 40, 41, 42
Cardinal numbers: 13; ordinal numbers 1st–31st: 79–81

Adverbs
End position adverbials with common prepositions: 9, 11, 14, 25–27, 44, 51, 70–73
too: 44, 63, 64, 66, 67

Connectives
and: 1, 3, 5, 17, 18, 35, 46, 48, 49, 56, 63, 79, 87, 88, 94; *but*: 31, 35, 51, 56, 57, 73, 89; *or*: 36–39, 43

Determiners
a + countable nouns and *the* + countable/uncountable nouns: throughout
that: 34; *these*: 40; *those*: 34, 40–42; *some*: 40, 66–68, 73, 87–88; *any*: 66–68, 77

Interrogatives
What . . .?: throughout; *What* (noun) *. . .?*: 19; *Where . . .?*: 9, 11, 12, 65, 68, 85; *Whose . . .?*: 81; *Which . . .?*: 52–55, 65, 78, 81 86; *Who . . .?*: 10, 45, 48; *How . . .?*: 1–3; *How many . . .?*: 13, 28, 78, 79, 81, 86, 89, 90; *How much . . .?*: 12

Nouns
Singular and plural countable nouns: throughout
Uncountable nouns: 16–18, 23, 24, 35, 43, 44

Prepositions
at, by, to, in, of, on, above, under, near, behind, with between: throughout

Pronouns
Personal: throughout
Impersonal: *it* 3, 82, 83, 86; *there*: 11, 13, 14, 57, 66–68, 78–79, 81, 83, 86, 94: *this*: 5, 15, 25, 26, 27, 62, 64; *these*: 4, 12, 40, 44–47; *some*: 66–68, 73, 77: *that*: 15, 21, 25, 26, 27, 36, 62–64; *those*: 40, 41, 46; *any*: 66–68, 77

Verbs
am, is, are: throughout; *have, has*: 14, 19–21, 23, 63, 66, 67; *can, ability*: 3, 4, 13, 21, 24, 28, 29–31, 35, 51, 68, 83, 85; *can*: asking permission: 23, 24, 34
Simple imperatives: throughout; negative imperatives: 33, 35, 52–55, 65
Present continuous: 1, 3, 10, 11, 34, 52, 58, 62
Simple present: 16–28, 40–42, 45, 48, 49, 70–73, 76, 77
be, have and *can*: throughout
Simple past: 82–92, 94

Word order
Simple affirmative and negative statements: throughout
Simple 'Yes/No', 'or' and 'Wh' questions: throughout